**Cla**

**Leai**

Ní mó
ar nó

Ar iarr
athnu

Gearr
choim

# SO, I'M SURE YOU'RE ~~WONDERING~~ WHAT'S THIS BOOK ~~ABOUT?~~

This book brings to light the trials and tribulations of parenthood that are inevitable but in a lighthearted, witty and refreshing way. Adding honesty combined with a touch of sarcasm to life not only brightens someone's day but makes it simpler - as parents it's always comforting to know that your struggle is not yours alone, and that there are many others out there who are facing the same challenges in parenthood. It's the ultimate mood lifter for parents all over the world and all you need is a sense of fun!

Give the Gift of Giggles

TO: _____

FROM: _____

Published by The Independent Publishing Network

Distributed by Truzees Ltd.
Copyright © at Truzees Ltd. All rights reserved
www.truzees.com

Design and illustration by Angela Mahon, Truzees Ltd.

Printed and bound by CPI Group (UK) Ltd.,
Croydon, CR0 4YY
First printing April 2016

Photography by Jeff Harvey
Photo credits: Jenny McCarthy, PhotosByJen p.73;
Jacqueline Taylor pp.76, 120; Jill O'Meara p.78;
Tony Gavin p.116; James Reese p.118; Dermot Byrne p.125

ISBN: 978-1-78280-739-1

## Agree and ignore

Graciously accept all parenting advice from others
with a polite smile and a nod. Then go and do
exactly as you had planned to do anyway.
Yes- including the advice from this book.

# CONTENTS

## Meet the Founder and Editor, Angela Mahon

Designer, Mum of one, Aunt to five.
Growing up, I was often told off for being a tad too truthful.

*www.truzees.com*

While I sat and rocked my newborn baby as he screamed, I found myself wondering why no one had told me what to really expect. There seemed to be a lack of discussion surrounding the true-to-life aspects and honest, stark reality of what parenthood would bring. No one had told me about the unconventional baby to toddler milestones that were inevitable. I wasn't aware that newborn babies would utilise the age-old savage method of 'sleep deprivation' torture, that the toddler would draw all over my cream leather chairs (with blue pen and on all four of them!), or that he'd say a naughty word at the most inappropriate of times. Sure, a baby is a wonderful gift but with them, babies bring an abundance of 'What the heck' moments.

What had been discussed and promoted was a bright, shiny veneer on real parenthood. Moreover, I received a total of six silver shiny frames as baby gifts as though to rub that concept in my face. Nowhere, did I see, hear or read a true reflection of the real process. At the very least, this information at the time, would have been beneficial and prepared me somewhat for the more challenging moments. I needed information from other mums who were in the trenches; buried deep in nappies and snotty noses to ensure me that as a parent I was doing just fine.

This book is a gift for a mother who is so deep in the trenches, she thinks that "luxury" is having an uninterrupted nap.

- Angela

## Meet our Writer and Editor, Nikki Lawlor

Newspaper columnist, writer of 'Life at Lawlors', Mum of three small humans, owner of one husband and two dogs.

*Follow 'Life at Lawlors' on Facebook and @nikkilawlor85 on Twitter*

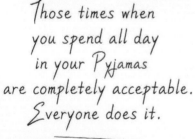

Those times when you spend all day in your Pyjamas are completely acceptable. Everyone does it.

A couple of years ago, I began writing about my day-to-day experiences of motherhood for numerous reasons; my children's behaviour seemed to make people laugh. I knew this from the response I received from the snippets shared about them on social media. It was suggested by many of my kind and encouraging friends to start to blog, and, as I'm clearly so easily influenced, I began to come around to that idea and think 'Yes- why not?'.

In time, I was fortunate enough to be offered my own tiny space in a local newspaper to publish my confused thoughts surrounding parenthood and the various antics that my children engaged in on a weekly basis. Overall, I tend to never write about the perfect family life. I feel this is completely unattainable for any of us. Instead, I write about the real, honest and true to life reality of it all; the embarrassments, the wobbles and the moments of doubt.

My hope for this book is that someone may read something that will make them smile. That they'll read something that they will nod along to, understand and empathise with. As cheesy as it sounds, I hope this book serves as a reminder that, while none of us are doing it perfectly, we are all doing our best.

- Nikki

# 20 TIPS TO KEEP YOU SANE IN THE EARLY DAYS

by Nikki Lawlor

## 1.

### Food, glorious food

Stock up on take away menus. Preferably from restaurants that deliver to your door.

## 2.

### Be kind to yourself

Whoever said you would get your figure back six weeks after giving birth was lying. You have just created an entire human. It's going to take longer than six weeks. Much longer.

## 3.

### Coffee is your friend

4am is no longer the middle of the night. 4am is now morning.

## 4.

### Your car is your friend

Babies tend to fall asleep a lot while driving in the car. Every parent has therefore, at one point, sat in a parked car for a lengthy period of time rather than wake their sleeping baby. Who cares if you're late or need to go inside – do you hear that?
Yes – it's total silence.

### Stocking up

Muslin cloths, burp cloths, whatever - you need
approximately one hundred of these. Stock up.

### How things have changed

Accept that 'we pulled an all-nighter' will never
again have the same meaning.

### Stretch marks

They aren't stretch marks, they're hero marks –
you've created a person in your body.
Wear with pride.

### Dreaded nappies

We have all put a nappy on backwards. No one is
judging you. If they are, they have probably never
had to change the nappy of a newborn baby.

## 9.

### Learning

Understand that NOBODY knows what they're doing in the beginning.

## 10.

### Invaluable life changing information

Those little folds on the shoulders of babygrow's are for FOLDING THE BABYGROW's down towards the bottom of the baby – not over the head in the event of a poo explosion. Honestly, this was only brought to my attention after toilet training three children and I still weep occasionally about all those days where I attempted to wipe poo off my beautiful new born baby's head...

## 11.

### Long haul flights

Accept that no one wants to sit next to you on a long haul flight anymore.

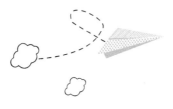

## 12.

### Feeling sad

Talk to someone if you feel sad. It's normal to be overwhelmed. It doesn't mean you love your baby any less than anyone else. We've all been there.

## 13.

### Unexpected visitors

In those early days, we have all kept the curtains closed and ignored the knocking from an unannounced, well intentioned caller. The house is a mess, you look like rubbish, you don't feel like making small talk and do you know what? It's absolutely fine!

## 14.

### Crying. The crying

Babies cry. It's what they do. Don't feel the need to remove yourself from anywhere because your baby is doing so. Anyone who objects to your baby crying has either never been related to a small child or has never been a small child themselves.

## 15.

### Little boys

Baby boys tend to pee as soon as you take their nappy off. Prepare to wipe urine off your walls. And your shirt- repeatedly.

## 16.

### First night out

Embrace the fact that, on that first night out you WILL call home approximately sixteen hundred times. It doesn't matter that you've probably left your small child with a relative who has raised five children of their own. It also doesn't matter that you're probably less than ten miles away. And that you've left the number of the local GP, hospital, dentist, vet and grocery delivery service. You're still going to do it. You don't need to. But you will.

## 17.

### Build an extension

With babies, comes a ridiculous amount of STUFF. Your living room will soon resemble properties from any given episode of 'Hoarders'.

## Self care

Babies can be all consuming - please ensure that you don't underestimate the importance of taking care of yourself. If you get a chance to have a break – take it and don't feel guilty for doing so.

## Weird habits that accompany parenthood

You are now about to start calling your significant other 'mom' or 'dad' to encourage your baby to do the same. It IS weird. Nonetheless, just roll with it.

## Things that set you off

In the early days, crying through advertisements for tea bags is normal.

SOON, YOU WILL REFER TO
COWS AS "MOO-MOO'S" AND TO
DOGS AS "WOW-WOW'S."

# MUM BEHAVING BADLY:

by Sophie White

# 10 TIMES THAT I WANTED TO PUNCH SOMEONE SINCE BECOMING A MOTHER

I'm not a particularly angry person, but prolonged sleep deprivation can really take its toll on a person's stocks of cheeriness. There is much discussion about what mothers really, really want for Mother's Day and I thought long and hard about this one.

I've come to the conclusion that what I would really like if the laws of time/physics/reality did not apply is this: I'd like to lash out at anyone who annoyed me. If only, just for one day I could lash out either verbally or physically I really don't mind which, and for there to be no consequences. Kind of a Groundhog Day set up whereby I'd have the satisfaction of releasing my rage without any long term consequences. I could do what I want, say what I want, essentially be Larry David for the day.

It's probably not the healthiest thing to wish for, but the heart wants what the heart wants. I think it would be a great release for all the times in the past year that I have refrained from punching people who have annoyed me.

Here are all the things I would've said if I were having my Groundhog Mother's Day:

## 1.

To the women (literally hundreds at this stage) who asked me if I was "feeding him myself":

"No, I've outsourced all his feeds to this amazing lactating cat I've got. Now go away and stop asking strangers about their tits."

## 2.

To my mother-in-law who asked "why is that child crying?" when my son was two weeks old and had been crying for the entire two weeks:

"I don't know, but your son implanted that thing in me, and now it's here you need to take at least some of the responsibility for this."

## 3.

To the woman who told me that I should try to get my non-sleeping son into a routine as if I had been completely rejecting the notion of a routine all this time. As if I haven't been methodically and precisely replicating the bedtime of the night before for the past 386 days:

There are no words...I might just kick her in the shins and run away.

To my neighbour's dog, who barks continuously as he walks past my house, four times every day:

"I hate you, I hate you, I hate you."

5.

To my childless friends who complain about how exhausted they are:

"F****cccccccckkkkkkk you! Come back to me after 16 months of broken sleep, dealing with another person's bodily functions and heavy lifting. Then we'll talk."

6.

To my co-diners at breakfast the other day:

"I'm sorry that my son dropping cutlery on the floor is causing you such grievous irritation, but giving him cutlery to drop, then handing it back to him, so that he can drop it once more is the trade off I have to make in order to sit here and enjoy my bloody Mary. So deal."

## 7

To the random women at the shops or in the street who feel the urge to tell me constantly "that child is tired" or "that child is hungry" or "that child is cold":

"Oh my god you are so right. These throwaway observations have proven that you're a better mother to him than I could ever be. Please, take him. Take him and give him the life that I could never give him."

**8.**

To my mother who made me build a fort out of menus the first time I breastfed in public:

"Get a grip. Our poorly constructed fort is more offensive then my breasts."

**9.**

To my husband who suggested that a playsuit three weeks postpartum was not my best look:

"I look better in a playsuit three weeks postpartum than you have EVER looked in a pair of shorts... and yes you are right, the playsuit is a no go."

## 10.

Finally to any of the many, many randomers who offered assistance or kind words over the past year:
**"Thanks" and \*sob\***

# HILARIOUS PARENTING TWEETS

"When you bump into the door and say 'sorry' to it.
#TiredMum."

- Truzees, @Truzees

"Children Should Be Seen & Not Heard

--a fairytale."

- Keep Meh & Carry On, @TheAlexNevil

# LIFE CHANGING TRAVEL FACTS

by Rose Jacobs

Did you know that the 100ml liquid rule doesn't apply to baby liquids? I'm not kidding. And no, it doesn't mean you can now sneak through your extra bottles of perfume and Chandon in the name of "baby liquid". But it does seriously change a few things if your child is still on the bottle.

Put simply, it means that when you are passing through customs (anywhere in the world, including Los Angeles!) and the security check requires you to declare all liquids, you simply pull out the bottles of liquid that are required for your baby's journey and identify it as such. If it isn't in a sealed container i.e, a poured bottle of milk, then the interesting thing that they are usually required to do is to run the bottles through a particular scan to test if it contains an explosive substance of any form, and then (this was the part that really threw me the first time, I thought they were taking the piss!) they ask you to sip a small amount of the liquid in front of them to prove it is edible. (Once again, another good reason why you shouldn't attempt to hide your extra duty free perfume using this method).

In saying that, I want to also point out that almost every international and most domestic airline I have travelled with have happily and promptly provided any milk and bottle top ups I have requested during flights, at no charge. If you require your own special milk (or breast milk etc) and don't want to rely on the airlines for it, then the air staff are also more than capable of storing your milk in the galley fridges for you too, since a long haul flight requires your milk to remain chilled (along with your state of mind).

Airlines have been around for a while. Long enough to know that a dilemma such as a hungry baby or a child with an explosive nappy is a potential threat to inflight safety, and as such, MANY INTERNATIONAL FLIGHTS STOCK EXTRA NAPPIES AND FORMULA IN CASE OF EMERGENCIES. Never a good idea to rely on this emergency stash, but good to know all the same. Think of it as your parachute.

## Interesting fact 2:

Next, the baby bjorn rule. It drives me nuts every time I have to pass through a customs security check point at an airport, and every airport has a different rule when it comes to the "baby bjorn" rule. This refers to whether or not they require you to remove your (often sleeping) angel from the baby bjorn, put it through the security conveyor belt (the bjorn, not the baby) and then re-attach baby to your bjorn two metres and one X-ray machine later. I am the first to agree that safety comes first and I am more than willing to oblige by any rules that mean we are all less likely to be blown up mid air, but it would make my day a lot easier if the airports across the globe (or even just the ones in Australia) could agree on the same protocol. However, because there are some airports that don't require you to remove the bjorn and sleeping baby (because it has no metal in it at all) I always make the effort to ask at each airport before I automatically remove it. Those few times when they wave you through are so, so worth it.

## Interesting fact 3:

Flushable wipes. Oh yes my friends, they exist. They can be found in your average supermarket (Woollies, Coles in Aus) in the toilet paper section (strangely not in the baby products area) and they come in the exact same travel friendly packaging as your regular Johnson & Johnson baby wipes. Only, they can be flushed!!!!! Wooohoooooo!!!!! No more man-handling poopy nappies in your left hand, poop covered wipes in your right hand, whilst precariously balancing your wriggling super cute baby above a teeny tiny, ecoli strewn airplane toilet. Flush and walk away!!

Being Australian, it is common practice to be handed an infant seatbelt as soon as you board a plane. (Domestic included). In fact, a plane is not permitted to take off if a child is not wearing a seatbelt, be it their own if they are older than two years of age, or the special separate one that attaches to yours so they are sitting on your lap for babies. So, you can imagine how odd it is when you board a flight, anywhere in America, for example, and the flight stewardesses say "a what sweetie?!" when you ask them for an infant seatbelt. I don't know the reasoning behind why they don't provide them (ahem, CHEAP airlines!!) but according to the safety regulations, you are also better off NOT STRAPPING YOUR INFANT INTO YOUR OWN SEATBELT as a back up option. Apparently, if in the event of an incident, the force of your own body would potentially crush your infant strapped inside your belt - which would be more damaging than the impact they would receive by being simply let to fly around the cabin. As I said, either way, I simply cannot understand why ANY airline would allow any passengers, especially the infants to travel without a seatbelt, but that's the way it is. And that's the reason why you can't strap them inside yours.

If your little one is of the age where he/she can sit patiently and engage in an iPad or portable DVD player etc of any form, then they must also (according to most airlines) have their own set of headphones. I learnt this the hard way on a flight from LA to CANCUN, Mexico. Two year old Isabella has recently discovered kids movies we downloaded to our iPad as a brilliant form of inflight entertainment. Much to our delight also!!! So you can imagine how frustrated we were when we were told she "had to have the device plugged into headphones or on silent" for the comfort of other passengers. Does anyone know a two year old who enjoys wearing small ear plugs?? And no, we didn't have a lovely set of children's head phones at hand. So, she simply had to watch Nemo on silent. Seriously.

So, they are some tips of the day. Again, they are things I've found out the hard way. If you've got any more to add, PLEASE email them through to hello@truzees.com. As the General in the kid's movie "Ants" would say, "It's for the good of the colony!"

# 5 SIMPLE TRUTHS FROM A FIRST TIME MAMMY

by Naomi Clarke

## 1.

The amount of things I now do with one hand is truly amazing. It's a skill I never knew I would be so good at. Washing out bottles, feeding the dog, opening the letter box, setting the table, (occasionally blogging!!!) yep…ALL one handed, whilst I carry Anabelle (or AB as we call her). I think I deserve an award!

## 2.

Your old body is gone…

I have dealt with countless women on personal shopping trips who have struggled with their new post-baby bodies. I never truly understood it until I had a baby myself.

Your body is incredible; I am beyond fascinated with how I carried Anabelle and made this perfect, adorable, human that she is. I stare at her little fingers and toes in awe. To do that, your body had to go through some SERIOUS changes and yes, now you look different, maybe your tummy sags, maybe your boobs are bigger, or smaller or not as perky, or maybe you can't lose those extra pounds you wish you could…to be the 'old' you. Who cares? Try not to be so hard on yourself. I know that is WAY easier said than done, but cut yourself some slack ladies – You created life!!! Give it time. My mum told me a few days post Anabelle's arrival, "Naomi, give yourself 6 months, just let time and nature take is course" and slowly but surely it is.

### Sleep when they sleep is not always as easy as it sounds

If I had a euro for every time I heard this I'd be swimming in a sea of Chanel bags and Jimmy Choos! This is not always just that easy. I do try and have the odd nap when I can, but someones got to do the laundry, pack the dishwasher, and do all the mundane things that have to be done!!!! Plus like a mad eijit I am trying to work on top of everything! And yes, as everyone likes to say 'don't worry about the house'…But dear Lord, mostly this place looks like a bomb went off!

### A shower, blowdrying your hair, painting your nails are all now luxuries

Yes, a shower. This is still a luxury, as for having time to properly blow dry my hair…ahhh gone be with the days! Now, it's like a war zone in here

when my hubby Cormac gets home from work, "quick take her, I need to shower". The weekends are my fav, as that's when Cormac is home and I can do nice things like go get my nails done and actually spend time drying my hair, but Monday to Friday it's pretty much a lot of dry shampoo and hope!! And don't even talk to me about my brows…
Oh lordy my brows!

## 5.

### Love

Last, but not certainly not least, you will experience a love so deep, a love like nothing you ever ever felt before. Now, nothing else matters, nothing at all matters, except Anabelle Ivy and her happiness and well being. It's the kind of love that just consumes every single inch of you and leaves you dreaming of her at night, even when you have just spent the day with her. Or flicking through photos of her when I go to bed at night, just to see that little face again.

It's the kind of love that you would lay down your own life and DO ANYTHING for her. So, you know what, f**k the dirty house, and your old skinny body and your unwashed hair, because this just surpassed it all and makes every single hard, seemingly never ending, teary day worth it.

# 9 THINGS YOU NEVER WANT TO HEAR AS A MOTHER WITH A COLICKY BABY

by Mary Widdicks

My first son was almost 8 weeks old before I realized he had colic. I hadn't spent much time around infants and I had no way of knowing whether all babies cried like my son, or if I was simply failing to calm him through lack of experience or some evolutionary failure of my maternal instincts. No matter how loud I sang, how energetically I danced, or how rhythmically I rocked him, my baby cried. He cried long and he cried loud and he cried constantly. But I wasn't a terrible mother; I wasn't a failure. There was nothing wrong with my son, and certainly nothing wrong with his lungs. We were just experiencing the phenomenon known as colic, like many other families out there, and knowing we weren't alone gave me the confidence to continue dancing even though it hadn't calmed him for the last hour and a half.

When my second son was born, I finally understood why sometimes other mothers would look at me strangely when I talked about the hours of crying through the night and the fact that my son would only sleep for half an hour at a time in the day. They had no idea what I was talking about. They had easy babies, and now I'd finally seen how the other half lived: Every moment of every day wasn't a struggle to survive. *Where's the fun in that?* Here are 10 things moms of the adorable bundles of shrieking joy never want to hear:

**1.**

*Have you tried... [insert obvious or cliché parenting advice here]? You mean I'm supposed to feed him when he's hungry?!?*

Come on, people. We're tired, but we're not THAT tired.

**2.**

*Man, I'm so tired today. I only got six hours of sleep last night.*

Really? I can't remember the last time I slept more than an hour and a half straight. Six hours of sleep sounds like a luxurious vacation. Suck it up.

**3.**

*Are you feeling OK? You look pale.*

If you ever ask this question of a new mother, you should probably run and hope she's too exhausted and anemic to catch you.

**4.**

*When is the last time you showered?*

I'm pretty sure it was a Tuesday... but what month?

Cherish these times/They're only young once.
Would you like to babysit?

You think this is bad? Just wait until he's 2.
That's super helpful. Why not just punch me in
the boob and run away?

I'm sure he'll grow out of it... in a few months.
Right now, a few hours seems like a lifetime. A
few months might as well be an eternity. But
thanks for the thought.

I remember this one time my baby cried for a
whole hour one night.
You just keep telling me all about that harrowing
experience. I'm gonna close my eyes for a
few minutes.

Weird, he never cries when I'm watching him.
Then he's all yours.

# 20 TIPS
# TO KEEP YOU SANE
# THROUGH THE
# TODDLER YEARS

by Nikki Lawlor

# 1.
## Potty Training

When your newly toilet trained toddler says they've "got to go", THEY HAVE GOT TO GO. Don't be me; don't think you can wait until the next public rest room is available. I've had my car seats, my hands, my knee and my cushions too wee stained to advise different...

# 2.
## On Repeat

Don't worry that through your continuous use of the words "No" and "don't touch" that your child may think one of the aforementioned is their actual first name. They won't. Ok scrap that – it's highly unlikely.

# 3.
## Tantrums

Know that the vast majority of people who are glancing your way when your toddler is having a total meltdown on aisle three of your local supermarket are not judging you. They aren't thinking awful things about your parenting. The majority ARE thinking "I remember when my Billy/ Jane did exactly the same thing".

## Dirty Text Messages Take On A Whole New Meaning

Accept that you are going to discuss the colour and consistency of poo more than you have ever done so in your life before. When toilet training our first born, my husband texted me a PICTURE of her first poo in the potty. At the time I was so happy. And so proud.

## House Arrest

Learn to work the stair gate lock. I once spent 45 minutes confined to the upstairs of my own house while waiting for help to arrive.

## Boys & Girls

It may be advisable to explain the difference between girls and boys to your older toddler before shocking them during a routine nappy change. My then sixteen month old son thought his new baby sister's penis had fallen off.

### 7.
### Toddlers

The majority of two year olds are the most unreasonable people you have ever met. Just know this.

### 8.
### Three Year Olds

The terrible twos are followed by the 'threenager' stage. Stock up on wine.

### 9.
### Appropriate Attire

Don't ask your toddler to dress themselves – regardless of how behind time you are. I once, after leaving out her clothes, asked my three year old to do so. She appeared in the kitchen dressed in: A pink princess nightdress, my purple shower cap, her father's navy polka dot tie and a pair of blue adult flippers. I kid you not. Although it admittedly adds to the comic value, it also adds to the time pressure.

## 10.
### Crayon Creations

Embrace the fact that your fridge door is now the new Louvre for baby artwork.

## 11.
### Cunning Compliments

Don't accept compliments too lightly from your small people. I've been told I'm beautiful and very clever by my cunning three year old, only to immediately be asked if she can stay up a little later that particular night.

## 12.
### Choose Your Words

Toddlers take everything literally. Learn to specify requests clearly and without sarcasm. I once told my then two year old to pee in my bedroom as I was using the main bathroom. I actually meant "pee in the toilet, in the ensuite, in my bedroom". Toddlers take things literally. You get the picture.

## 13.

### Mispronunciations

Create your own translator for your toddler. Write
this stuff down if needs be. Mispronunciations are an
adorable and humorous bonus to having kids. Some
in my house include: 'other pants' (underpants),
'angina' (vagina), and 'Elephants' (infants).

## 14.

### First day of school

Even the most hardcore and unemotional ones
of us will, on THAT first day of school, find
ourselves at home, crying and drinking countless
cups of tea whilst wondering where on earth those
last five years went. It flies. It really does. Accept
you are no longer the toughie you thought you
once were.

## 15.

### B*llshit

Ignore the continuous social media pictures from
other parents, with their perfectly cleaned houses
and additionally perfectly turned out children –
they have posted this picture and made it public
because it's a rarity – we've all done it. They are
the same as you. In four seconds, their house will
too resemble the aftermath of a hurricane.

## 16.
### Toilet Privacy

Accept that you no longer have privacy on trips to the bathroom. Peeing, showering and bathing without at least one small child accompanying you and staring at you throughout with a running commentary are a thing of the past.

## 17.
### Bed Wetting

After a middle of the night bed wetting accident, don't feel guilty when you throw a towel down on the mattress instead of changing the sheets. We've all done it.

## 18.
### Be prepared

Keep spare clothes in the boot of your car. At all times.

## 19.
### Life has changed

Accept that 90% of your life now will comprise of you screaming "please will you just get your shoes on NOW!!"

## 20.

### Tardiness

Set all your clocks forward fifteen minutes. You will always be late.

# HILARIOUS PARENTING TWEETS

"Parenthood is a journey except it's just traveling from room to room putting away the same toys all day long."

– OneFunnyMummy , @OneFunnyMummy

"Hurry up and finish your Red Bull kids, your mom will be here in 15 minutes to pick you up."

– Matthew Griffin, @Matt_The_1st

# MUM BEHAVING BADLY:

by Sophie White

# 10 TIMES A TOTAL F*CKING -STRANGER- KNEW HOW TO RAISE MY CHILD

If you have ever gone out in public with your child, then you most likely have been on the receiving end of some unsolicited advice.

The first time it happened to me I was pretty surprised. It would never occur to me to tell some total randomer what to do when it comes to, well, virtually everything. Unless they were accidentally backing their car over another human being.

I would probably stay far, far away from interfering. However, what I didn't realise was that by becoming a mother I was apparently inviting the world in to critique my parenting efforts.

## 1.

"That child is tired."

Okaaaayy. Thanks for the info?

## 2.

"You really should breastfeed, it's the best thing for a baby you know."

REALLY? Do you actually think that in nine months of pregnancy and six months of parenthood that I've never heard that little nugget of wisdom?

## 3.
### "That's Wind."

How? HOW do you know it's wind? For all you know he just burped. Okay, I know it's probably wind but c'mon it's always wind. You're stating the obvious.

## 4.
### "Does he not have a soother?"

If he had a soother, someone else would be saying "Dummies ruin their teeth and cause obesity."

## 5.
### "That child's too old for a bottle."

And I'm too old to be told what to do by a hatchet-faced hag.

## 6.
### "He's very small are you giving him a bit of formula to top him up?"

I have issues with the phrases "topping up", "sleeping through" and "in my day", that is all.

## 7.

"That child shouldn't be eating crisps."

Okay, I know this is true to some extent but LEAVE me alone. I am preparing nutritious meals ninety f*cking nine per cent of the time. What you are seeing here is a SNAPSHOT of our lives so back off.

## 8.

"Those teething beads are dangerous."

Yes I think I might strangle you with them.

## 9.

"Spare the rod, spoil the child."

I am giving in to everything this child demands because I'm too tired to discipline today.

## 10.

"Has he no socks?"

No, despite having bought exactly one million pairs of socks I couldn't find any in the chaotic hell hole that is our house. I bow down before your wisdom. Please just take him, give him the life that I can't give him.

# 10 THINGS I HAVE NO PATIENCE FOR SINCE MAKING A HUMAN

by Sophie White

Harsh as this sounds, once you're making your own people other people (unless they are really fun or Tom Hardy) seem somehow surplus to requirement.

While before I would smile and nod along with whatever minor irritant I was faced with, now I find my tolerance levels have totally plummeted and I just can't be bothered with people or things who are annoying me.

Disclaimer: I realise that I sound like a b*tch... That is all.

## 1.

### Restrictive or uncomfortable clothing

Once you've gone elasticated it can be hard to go back. Even though my body has returned to a rough approximation of person-shaped and I feel obliged to wear garments with traditional waistbands, I still treat myself to a few "elasticated days" every week.

## 2.

### Strangers who, while referring to my child, start sentences with the words "That child..."

"That child" has absolutely ZERO to do with you.

## Anyone (other than me) moaning about being "tired" or "stressed"

I know that I sound like a total b*tch but that's just what being tired and stressed does to a person.

## The word "judgement"

I think a lot of this "judgement" is in our heads and we all need to get on with not giving a sh*t about what the woman minding her own business over there might think about how we choose to feed, water or clothe our babies. There's a lot of people around feeling judged these days and I just wanted to categorically say I'm too concerned with what I'm potentially doing wrong, to judge you. And likewise I will assume that you certainly can't summon the will to care about me either.

Unless you are literally getting your infant tattooed, I think you're doing a great job. If you are getting your baby tattooed, then I admit it, I am judging you.

## 5.

### People writing open letters of the "Dear Mum on the iPhone..." variety

It's always been a pet peeve of mine but I admit since making the human and officially hitting a level of zero tolerance for bullsh*t, I have been fighting an urge to write an open letter of my own. This is how it would go; "Dear Mum writing an open letter... F*ck off."

## 6.

### Staying up late

It's off the menu. Unless it's a really, REALLY good night, I just can't say that it is worth it anymore. For the childless, every hour out later is another hour of unadulterated fun, for me it's an hour less sleep and brings me ever closer to being a strong contender in a Keith Richards lookalike contest – I wear my exhaustion in the face.

## 7.

### Post-baby body selfies

Does this require an explanation? Okay here's one: It's my body, I'm filling it with cupcakes and no "inspiring" post-baby body selfie is going to stop me.

## Cutting down on wine

Before I was always trying to maintain my person-shaped figure and looking out for my health. Now that I'm saddled with The Child and The Man, I've decided to go full-tilt into letting myself go. It's liberating. All I have left is to cultivate my wine gut and indulge in emotional wine-fuelled weeping about how much I love my baby (and to a lesser extent The Man).

## Lengthy sexual encounters

Who has the time? Or inclination? Things have veered so far into platonic around our house that The Man is threatening to impose a sex schedule. I asked if he would be making it on an SExcel Spread sheet. He was not amused.

## Being nice to virtually anyone

See points 2, 3 and 10.

# A FEW THINGS I'VE LEARNT
# SINCE BECOMING A MAMA

Patience, I wouldn't be a naturally patient person
but when it comes to Josh a whole new found
world of patience occurs.

Sleep, or lack of it. You learn to survive on
little sleep.

Interpreter, I am a top notch toddler jibber
translator.

Cartoons, get us through an early weekend start.

Planning, I was always a planner but being a
mama brings it to a whole new level.

Resilience, I've learnt to bounce back from things
at the speed of light.

- by Mama Felton aka Kelly

53

# 50 TIPS
# TO KEEP YOU SANE
# THROUGH IT ALL

by Nikki Lawlor

### 1.

Ensure you check the full ingredient list when purchasing a shop bought cake. I have previously bought the most beautiful and expensive cake for my four year old's birthday only to realise, upon taking it home that it's almost entirely made from coffee.

### 2.

**&^%&(*)*

Be extra mindful of the more 'colourful' language you may use. At a recent check up appointment, my four year old took it upon herself to interrupt her Doctor, mid sentence to tell him "Mommy, said a very, very bad word when she spilled coffee in the car this morning"

### 3.

Your phone

Never trust your kid to play a game on your phone. I once caught my four year old logged in as me, on a social media site – 'liking' statuses and pictures of people I don't like.

## 4.
### Imitation

Mind your manners and your actions. Your children will always copy you because they think you're pretty wonderful. I know this because I once discovered my four year old son standing in my sitting room, wearing my heels while holding an (empty) coffee cup in his hands. In a VERY squeaky voice and, while wagging his finger at his sisters, he was declaring "I don't care who started it guys, I AM FINISHING IT!!" <blush>

## 5.
### School

Prepare for the younger one to BEG to go to school. And for the older one to pretend to be sick to stay home.

## 6.
### Hobbies

Your older child is likely to plead with you to allow them to take up a certain musical instrument/ dance class or sport before ditching it completely five minutes later. They'll only do this once you've bought all the gear required. Attempt to exercise patience.

## 7.

### Bed Acrobatics

Don't panic when you complete a late night head count and can't find your two year old in his bed. He's at the bottom of it or he's under it. Failing that – he's in your bed. I once found my three year old in my bed at 10pm. I asked what she was doing there. She looked at me as though I was completely stupid before replying "Em.. Mommy; I LIVE here..."
I'm an idiot.

## 8.

### Wise Words

Children are wiser than we sometimes give them credit for. I once thoughtlessly made an off the cuff remark about needing to 'man up'. My nine year old corrected me – declaring 'I think you meant you need to WOman up, mam – that way, you'll be REALLY tough.'"

## Kids are IT experts

Children are really useful. This week alone, my four and five year old have helped me work the record function on our cable TV, the household Wi-Fi AND the games console...
Utilise their skills.

## You are old now

Regardless of what age you are when you have your children, they will consider you old. I had my first at twenty. She thinks I'm ancient. When I was twenty seven, she once asked if there was electricity or running water back then in the olden days...when I was young.

## Clothes

When separating laundry, be conscious of separating your clothes and the children's clothes properly. Last year, I spent 20 whole minutes bitching about the fact that I couldn't get a pair of jeans up past my bum. Cue the mandatory vows to never eat again/ to diet the following week/ to start running. I even mentally planned meals for the next day. You know the type; healthy, tasteless, soul destroying stuff. Turns out they were my nine year old daughter's jeans. I wasn't fat – I was just incredibly stupid! (Yay!)

## 12.

### Phone calls

Possibly inform all your friends and family members that the reason every single phone call with you now sounds like you are strangling a cat in the background whilst occasionally shouting to the same cat to please be quite, is not because you're doing so, it's because you now share your home with small children.

## 13.

### Leaving the house

Make your peace with the fact that a quick trip to the supermarket will now take more organisation, planning and preparation than all of your previous child free holidays abroad. Or an entire military exercise for that matter.

## 14.

### Sleep or lack thereof

Accept that sleep deprivation makes you stupid. It will pass. My oldest is almost ten. It's going to happen soon. Any day now...it's going to happen.

## 15.

### Nursery Rhymes

Learn the words to nursery rhymes again. Honestly – you won't believe how much you've forgotten. You won't ever forget them in adulthood, mind. Why? Because you'll be asked to sing the same song every 17 seconds for the next 10 years.

## 16.

### Cosmetics

Do not leave your make up lying around unattended. Should you do so, I guarantee you will find your small child more made up than Liz Taylor.

## 17.
### Thieves

Do not leave your keys lying around. If too late;
they are down the back of a radiator OR they are
in a toy box. Check now. Tell me I'm wrong.

## 18.
### Dirt

Kids get dirty. There is weight in the old saying
'dirty kids are happy kids'. Let them acquire grass
and mud stains.

## 19.
### Showers

Shaving, exfoliating and buffing in the shower
are likely to be a thing of the past. Be grateful on
the occasions you exit the shower clean. Embrace
your inner scruffiness.

## 20.
### Guilt

At one point its likely you'll accidently injure your child – by cutting their nail too short or by bumping their head off something. You will feel awful. Just know you aren't the first parent to do this and you won't be the last. My mother once closed the car door on my finger when I was six. Twenty four years later, I still bring it up – just to be an asshole.

## 21.
### Eating nice things

A small child can hear a biscuit packet being opened from as much as 30 feet away. They also possess a skill enabling them to sniff cake out from a considerable distance. You will never have a foodie treat again without having to share. I advise finding something delicious that you like that your kid doesn't. That way you'll win.

## 22.
### Your car

Your car is going to be a disgusting mess for the next 10 years. Don't offer lifts to anyone.

## 23.
### Babysitting

If you are fortunate enough to have grandparents in your life, be nice to them. Buy them stuff. Tell them their hair looks pretty. They are great for babysitting.

## 24.
### Magical Powers

You are actually magic as a parent. Do you know how I know this? Kissing an injury on your small child IMMEDIATELY makes it better. I don't know how, it just does. Magic!

## 25.
### Working outside of the home/ Working inside of the home

Going back to work is ok. Staying at home is ok. You know what's best for your family, yourself and your child. For Christ's sake – just do what makes you all happy.

## 26.

Accept that you will now cry and feel incredibly sad after hearing or seeing anything negative that relates to children. Even those you don't know. You're a parent now. It comes with the territory.

## 27.

Flowers

Children tend to pick flowers. So don't bother to plant them.

## 28.

Invisible Friends

Ensure you set an extra place at dinner and that you have an accompanying additional dish for same. Your small child may have an invisible friend visiting and we don't want to appear unwelcoming. As a side note, please be careful not to sit on said invisible friend.

## 29.
### Santa

Don't threaten your kids with 'Santa' in July.
You'll curse the day. Why? Because that's 5 long
months you'll be forced to listen to repeated
requests on Christmas wish lists.

## 30.
### Harsh truths

Retain your sense of humour and try to become
more hardened to honesty. My children have,
on numerous occasions now, pointed out that
'mommy has a very squishy, wobbly tummy'.
I, in return, have pointed out to each of them that
that's their fault.

## 31.
### Romance

Accept that every romantic anniversary/ birthday
or 'for the hell' meal will now likely include
a highchair in the middle of you both, with a
small person therein squealing with laughter and
robbing from both your plates.

## 32.
### Nicknames

Understand that you and your close relatives
will adopt odd nicknames for your new
offspring. Sometimes, when speaking about
the little people in your life, you will use these
nicknames in public, with colleagues or with
mere acquaintances. They won't 'get it'. You WILL
sound strange. I've heard (and used myself):
Little Roo, Boo-boo, Squidge, Spud, Stinkweed,
Donnakawanaka, Chubbachops, Uddy Buddy,
Pickle chops, Doodle, Scrapy Miss Kissy Knickers
and Pudding to name but a few.

## 33.
### Snap happy
Take too many pictures.

## 34.
### Out and about

Understand that should you find yourself out
and about and child free, you WILL answer any
random child's call of 'MOM?' It's natural
and instinctive.

Prepare yourself to no longer have any household secrets. My children have told both their childminder and teachers respectively of every mishap, argument, accident or embarrassing incident that has ever taken place at our house. The classroom assistant often looks at me sympathetically.

## 36.
### Why though?

Prepare yourself to be asked "why?" approximately six hundred times a day for at least five years. If you don't know why, make something up. It's easier.

## 37.
### Child development

Try not to compare developmental milestones between siblings or your child's achievements with the children of friends and acquaintances. They will all generally catch up with each other eventually.

## 38.

### Freedom

Know that your first trip to the supermarket alone, without children is like escaping Alcatraz unfollowed. You will feel a ridiculous amount of freedom whilst browsing the cereal aisle.

## 39.

### There's no escaping the fact

It's highly likely that, despite your previous vows to yourself, you will turn into your own parents. All those things you said you'd never say? You will find yourself saying exactly those things. "Cos I said so, that's why!"

Cringe if you will, object if you wish – it's going to happen.

## 40.

### Bad behaviour

No child IS bad or naughty. Sometimes their behaviour is. Make sure you vocalise the difference to them.

## 41.
### Treasure the treasured

Try to record those 'firsts' and milestones. Your child WILL ask questions about what they were like themselves as a baby when they're a little older and its lovely to have the answers for them.

## 42.
### Love

You know you love them above and beyond all else but remember to tell them this. Tell them you love them at every possible opportunity. Overkill if you must. You'll regret it if you don't.

## 43.
### Messy homes

Your house will never, ever be clean again. By all means tidy continuously to disprove this opinion but I'm right. Remember if anyone visits to judge the condition of your home and not to see you, well, then they shouldn't be welcome anyway.

## A forever position

Parenthood doesn't end when they turn eighteen and reach adulthood. They will be your baby forever. When they are fifty and they have a head cold, you will worry. My grandmother has shown me this.

## Expectations

Lower your expectations. The pre-baby intentions of "MY child will never do that." And "I will never do that with MY kid" are about to go out the window.

## Being quoted

Be careful of conversations that take place in the vicinity of little ears. Even if you think they aren't listening.
"My mommy said that you are an idiot.."
Kids are scarily honest.

Try not to feel guilty about everything.

Children squeeze toothpaste in the most inefficient way but you can't end the relationship or break up with them because of it. Unfortunately.

**49.**

Know that obliviously watching the cartoon channel for fifteen minutes after all children have left the room is normal. Embrace your inner love of animations.

**50.**

Enjoy them. It flies by.

# TRUE TO LIFE
# PARENTHOOD

A collection of stories and quotes from
TV personalities and parents alike

"I've had an infant on my breast since 5pm
and it's the only place she doesn't scream.
Love the shattered one."

- Leigh Arnold, Actress, Ireland

"Bella was born 3 months premature, she was tiny and she had to be wrapped up very warm all of the time. She was less than 6 months old when I went back to work. I returned home one day, Paul had a day off so he had taken her out to show her off to all his single, childless friends (really he couldn't just leave her at home as he swanned about town on his day off). When I got home, she was propped up on the sofa with a pair of her tights on her head. I asked Paul why she was adorning such a fashion item. He replied that he couldn't find her hat so he had to keep her warm somehow. He had brought our daughter into town wearing tights on her head. Only a Dad would be so resourceful!"

– Niamh Hogan, Holos Skincare, Ireland

**"I was feeling broody** and said I would love another baby. Two days later, Holly hadn't slept and I thought **'Right, I'm getting goldfish.'"**

– Lucy Kennedy,
Radio and TV Presenter,
Ireland

## The things kids do

"So all little boys love to get naked, my son went through this phase at the same time as being toilet trained! One sunny afternoon I had the balcony door open airing the apartment. While sorting clothes in the bedroom a small naked boy wandered into the room. Nothing too unusual there you say? Well what I discovered later that afternoon was not only had he gotten naked himself but when I went to close the balcony door low and behold I found a large brown lump on it! Yes ladies and gentleman my child had a poop on the balcony while completely naked! Needless to say I avoided all the neighbours for several months."

- Sarah, Ireland

## Stay at home mama

"Before I became a mother, I wrongly was under the impression that stay at home mothers had it made. What could be better, I thought, than staying at home all day with your little darlings, not having to conform to strict time keeping to make it to work on time? Essentially, I thought stay at home mothers were their own boss. Oh how wrong I was!"

– Fiona, Dolly Dowsie, Ireland

"When I became a mum I put a lot of pressure on myself to be perfect to give my baby the best start in life and I had this idea in my head that breastfeeding would just come naturally to me. When it didn't work out for me I felt like such a failure but after talking with my family and various breastfeeding coaches and nurses I realised that I wasn't a failure, that at the end of the day a happy Mom makes for a happy baby."

- Michelle Doherty, Actress & TV presenter, Ireland

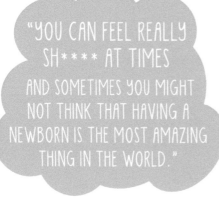

"YOU CAN FEEL REALLY SH**** AT TIMES AND SOMETIMES YOU MIGHT NOT THINK THAT HAVING A NEWBORN IS THE MOST AMAZING THING IN THE WORLD."

- Rebecca Judd, TV Presenter, Australia

"My least favourite memory of travelling the globe with very small children is one that has traumatised me for life. I experienced something of a panic attack (for the first time in my life) while stuck in a window seat on a flight from London to L.A. with my 18 month old daughter on my lap and the plane was stuck on the tarmac for three hours before takeoff. Isabella decided to experience a bout of projectile vomiting. I sat there, covered head to toe in vomit, unable to leave my seat or climb over the two passengers next to me, a child screaming and convulsing as if possessed on my lap. I actually considered pretending to be a security risk just so I could escape this scenario. And yet, two years later, I have since travelled a huge chunk of the world, with two kids in tow… and I'm still married! The moments, when they do go right, of seeing the beauty of the world, with your babies by your side, is indescribably beautiful."

– Rose Jacobs,
TV presenter,
Australia

### Beauty tip - because we need them

"Eyelash extensions are great - Some good under eye concealer is always good for hiding the dark circles!"

– Laura Hamilton, TV presenter UK

### "Babies don't get the whole extra hour in bed thing, do they?"

– Karen Koster, TV presenter, Ireland

### Bath time is just not the same

"My little man, Charlie (3 years old) and I were having a bath together last week. Beforehand, I had been wondering if maybe he was starting to get too old to have baths with his mummy. With this in mind, I used a face cloth to cover myself in the water. As children tend to, he quickly sensed I was hiding something and wanted to 'have a look' under the facecloth. I told him, 'No sweetheart, it's private.' His response made me cry laughing, 'I WANT TO SEE THE PIRATE!', he roared. The innocence."

– Marissa Carter, Cocoa Brown, Ireland

"When I went for the X-Factor audition, my daughter came with me. She had bought me a camp chair and a flask, made some tea and sandwiches and sat there with me in the freezing cold. A few times I wanted to go home and she wouldn't let me. To be honest, she was more nervous than I was - you've got to remember, she was looking at her 50 year old mother who was auditioning for this internationally televised show and was probably saying to herself 'I hope my mammy doesn't make a show of herself...and me.' But she was behind me 110%. At the time, my arthritis was killing me and there we were in a queue of thousands all running to get past the barriers. I said to her "I can't keep up with all these girls". With that, she shot off with my deck chair and the big bag full of tea and sandwiches and flew through the crowd with me hobbling behind her so that we could get to the top. Looking back, it was a hilarious moment and I'll never forget it."

– Mary Byrne, Singer-songwriter, Ireland

### Diplomacy

"Parenthood is the art of diplomacy – saying "would you like your hair washed before or after tea?" without acknowledging there may also be a third option…"

– Liz Earle, Author & broadcaster, UK

"Your parenting is the best parenting for your child and if you try to compare yourself to others, you will fall short."

– Kate Ceberano, Singer, Australia

"We are out of the **trenches** and onto the **main battle field**."

– Colette Fitzpatrick
TV Presenter, Ireland

– Sarah, UK

– Bobby & Hayley, Ireland

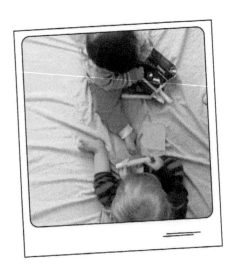

MUMS SANITARY THINGYS

– Catherine & Benny,
Ireland

"Beware...kids just LOVE Sudocrem and Vaseline."

– Sheena Lavin, Ireland

Beware of a tot that's too quiet!

– Jeff, father of two, Ireland

"My daughter really loves butter!!!
She went mental when I took it away after
taking a big bite!!!"

– Jennifer Doule, Ireland

Kids say the cutest things.

My son just asked me,
"Mom, who will make our lunches
if you're ever in the hospital?"

- @sarcasticmommy4

"Kids + paint + daddy's supervision = carnage!!"

– Victoria Houston, GB

Life isn't perfect but my kids are.

Clare, mother of three, Ireland

# TO HELL IN A HANDBAG: WHY MOTHERS CAN'T HAVE NICE THINGS

by Mary Widdicks

"It's designer." My husband beamed at me with such pride you would have thought he'd tanned the leather of the handbag himself with his own blood, sweat, and tears.

I turned the large grey bag over in my hands, admiring the luscious purple lining and shiny metal buckle. The chrome reminded me of the hood ornaments on really expensive cars, only it was nicer than any car I'd ever owned.

As a fashion neophyte, I was completely baffled by how, over the next few weeks, my new purse elicited several compliments, numerous envious gazes, and a fair amount of drool from passersby.

I could get used to this type of attention, I thought to myself as I caressed my new prize with the tender affection of a mother swaddling her new baby. Why had I resisted haute couture for so long?

Then I remembered.

As a mother of three small children, I discover a myriad of juicy surprises on and around my person every day. In this way, having children is not much different than having kittens, except cats at least have the decency not to deposit the dead mouse in your bra or stick the headless bird to the back of your yoga pants.

However, with children you have not only to act impressed and grateful for these "gifts," but you also have to store them somewhere convenient so that they may be produced the instant they are demanded at a later, unspecified date. At least once a week I embark on a grueling, life-altering pilgrimage to Target: my infant clinging to my shirt so tightly that my tattered nursing bra is bared for all the world to see, my toddler resting on my other hip smashing his half eaten banana in my face, and my four-year-old pulling the hem of my shirt, urging me to walk faster toward the toy aisle so he can beg and plead with me to buy him yet another tiny object that will turn up in my laundry the next week.

Sometimes there just isn't anywhere to deposit half a gooey, rejected banana that, should I throw it away, would therein be revealed as my toddler's only reason for existing.

So I lovingly wrap the slimy fruit in a tissue and place it in my flashy purse.

There are days when I remember at the last minute that our dogs are due for their yearly ritual of emptying my entire bank account and I end up stalking the dogs through the patch of grass outside the vet's office with a plastic bag in one hand, both leashes in the other, the baby strapped to my chest and the older kids playing dodge the poop.

So I stash the bag, which is now literally filled with a steaming pile of feces, in my fashionable purse. Then there are the treasure hunts my boys approach with such unbridled enthusiasm and naive wonder that I don't have the heart to tell my toddler that his "rock" is really a petrified goose turd or that his "leaf" is nothing more than a faded wrapper for an unidentifiable chocolate bar.

So I collect them and file them away in my exquisite handbag beside the acorns, twigs, and grass clippings my kids have already squirreled away for posterity.

Let's face it, I'm a mom, and no matter how delicately I handle my chic new purse it will inevitably fill up with sandy matchbox cars, leaky squeezy pouches, soiled underpants, diapers, and more snotty tissues than I ever thought possible.

I am every buttery-soft, hand-stitched, trendy bag's worst nightmare; my photo should be on the wall of every Neiman Marcus in the continental U.S.

Of course I loved the fleeting feeling of pride when I realized I was carrying something beautiful and desirable, and for a while I cringed every time my kids spilled their juice near it or left an uncapped marker inside. Then I realized that there was no point owning a purse that I was too afraid to use or pretending that my life wasn't filled with all the gooey, slimy, smelly, sticky joys that find their ways into my bag.

So maybe I can have nice things, as long as I accept that the real treasures in my life come from the three little monkeys who drool, snot, and climb all over me (and my purse) every day, and not some big-name designer. The best way I can enjoy my new purse is not to parade it, flawless and empty, through the grocery store, but rather to fill it with the things that make my family happy.

Even if some of those things stain.

# THINGS YOU'LL ONLY UNDERSTAND IF YOU'RE THE PARENT OF A TODDLER

Walks in the park with your little one can sometimes be heartwarming (feeding the ducks) and other times hell (trying to jump in and swim with them).

The theme tune to their favourite TV show will be the song you can't get out of your head.

You are delighted with the fact that they now chatter non stop however their brutal honesty knows no bounds and there's nothing you can do about it.

There is nothing more mortifying than telling your child that there are strictly no snacks allowed before dinner, and then them catching you with a mouthful of cake.

– by Jennie Dennehy

# N TO THE O TO THE NOOOOO!

Now that the words are coming thick and fast from both the minis, it seems we've entered the dreaded "Second No" phase. This is similar to the "First No phase" where the negatives spew forth from the cherub lips of your little darlings like in the following all too common exchange:

Small child "Mummy, drink!"

Me: "Would you like milk?"

Small child: "No!"

Me: "Would you like juice?"

Small child: "No!"

Me: "Would you like water?"

Small child: "Noooooo!!!"

Me: "Would you like a kick up the bum?"

That last one is said in my mind..sometimes. No, the "Second No Phase" refers to the refusing to acquiesce to the wills of a small child, which usually occurs once they have mastered a certain amount of vocabulary-usually all of their favourite things. It is most prevalent in tired and stressed out parents as they attempt to navigate the potentially loaded supermarket aisles while doing the weekly shop.

"Mummy, ice cream?"

"No!"

"Cakes?"

"No!"

"Chips??"

"No!"

"Biscuits?"

"Noooooooo!!!"

It seems Mini has come up with her own novel way to get what she wants. Today, after refusing to give her ice cream at the umpteenth plea, she turned on her heel and fled to her happy place, or the outside to you and me. As I was sorting out laundry, the following words floated up through the open bedroom window to me:

Mini: "Ice cream?"

Mini: "Yes please!!"

Mini: "Ok!"

Say what you will about the little lady, she is nothing if not determined. I nearly gave in to her heart felt request but refrained due to it only being 9:45 in the morning. It's only a matter of time before she'd have chipped away at my remaining parental resolve not to have ice cream for breakfast.

- by Aedin Collins

# HIDE AND SEEK GUIDE

Everyone knows the rules for playing 'hide and seek' – or do they??? Here's the guide for playing with a toddler:

You need:
2 players (a very patient adult and a very excited toddler)
One or more places to hide

Traditionally the seeker should close their eyes while the other player hides; this rule goes out the window. The parent should help their child to find a good hiding place and tell them to wait quietly. Ignore the fact that this should 'give the game away'.

Take the opportunity to count to thirty. Although your child has already found a place to hide this little break will give you ample time for a few glugs of coffee and to shove a biscuit in your mouth.

Important: do not crunch your treat loudly! This could result in the child running out from their 'hiding place' and demanding one too.
Once the time is up shout 'Ready or not, here I come!'

Chances are this will result in a fit of giggles and perhaps even more helpfully 'I'm here! I'm here!' Not that you needed reminding…

Use your best acting skills to ignore this revelation and attempt to find them in a few other locations, each time seeming more and more puzzled.

It's now time for the big reveal – creep over to their position and in your most surprised voice shout 'There you are!'

If they're pleased with how the game has gone they'll probably want an encore and that means repeating the whole thing again EXACTLY THE SAME. The first hiding place worked a treat so of course they'll want to hide there again.

Usually each player takes it in turns to hide; not in this case. Your toddler must hide EVERY TIME.

Complete the steps over and over until you start craving wine instead of coffee…

by Jennie Dennehy

# CHILDREN ARE PSYCHIC

"I didn't do it!"

Famous last words, right?

When my younger daughter, Destruction, says those four little words to me, deep down I want to believe her. Yet the instant they leave her lips I know they really translate to: "*Yes I did it, Mother Dearest. I did it, indeed. I don't want to tell you the truth about what I did because according to my latest calculations there's roughly a 3% chance of you getting angry but the odds are increasing at a staggering rate of 8.2 freakawatts per second!*"

I tucked my girls into bed, left their room and prepared myself for a cozy, quiet evening. Perhaps I'd watch some television. I brewed a cup of tea, gathered a blanket, and I found the remote control. I did not, however, find the case that contains my glasses.

After searching everywhere I had been in the house, it occurred to me that perhaps I should question the two little bundles of joy who were snuggled up beneath cozy comforters, much like the way I could be curled up with my own warm blanket in the living room.

I knew they'd still be awake. I went to their room to begin the inquisition.

"Have either of you seen my glasses case? I keep it on the end table in the living room. Did either of you see it or put it somewhere?"

My older daughter looked bewildered, obviously having no idea what had happened to it.

Destruction sat up, wide eyed and considerably alarmed. "I didn't do it!"

I said, "Oh…kay. But did you see it anywhere?"

She said, "Let me think… Maybe you should check the drawer of the nightstand in the guest room. I think I saw it there."

Stifling laughter, I walked directly across the hall to investigate her claim. And wouldn't you know it? They were exactly where she said they would be.

by Alison Huff

# KIDS, STOP MESSING WITH ME

by Nikki Lawlor

Today, my 2 year old has requested a cold, hot
bottle of milk.
I've asked her which she would like – a hot OR a
cold one.
She tells me she would like a cold, hot one.
I'm glad we've cleared this up.

Today my 3 year old is upset because her ice
cream smells cold.

Today, my 5 year old is angry with me because I
won't tell him any bad words.

Today, my 5 year old is crying because I can't
make today be tomorrow.

Today, my 3 year old is annoyed that she has
'nuts and bolts' in her leg.
She has pins and needles.

I'm preparing dinner and ask my 5 year old if he would like a raw carrot.
"No thanks" comes the reply "I would like mine not cooked"

I'm trying to explain daylight saving time to a 2 year old without success "but I can't go to bed, mommy! Outside says it's still morning time...

This morning for breakfast, my 3 year old daughter would like a piece of toast that has not been toasted.
My 5 year old son would like dinner.

I'm sitting at my dressing table putting on my face and notice a small child to my right with her face pinned to the mirror making a series of odd expressions. Curiosity gets the better of me and I ask "Kate, what are you doing? "
"I'm practising being mad and angry" she replies "but my face just keeps doing happy and laughing ALL of the time.. " she sighs.

After a brief hospital stay, I arrive home. My 5 year old cuddles up next to me on the couch to welcome me back. "I'm glad your home, Mommy. I was worried" he tells me.
I feel loved and wanted.
"Aw, you're very sweet" I tell him "You didn't need to worry".
"But I was worried" he says "I was worried about who was going to make me sandwiches and cut my toenails..."

My 5 year old: "Daddy, we're getting a cake and candles for you and its your birthday but don't tell you because its a secret and a surprise, ok?"
Excellent. A career in secret services destined here I suspect.

Today, my 4 year old is annoyed with me because I insist on turning both left and right when driving my car. He's trying to drink his juice back there and I'm being unreasonable.

#KidsStopMessingWithMe

99

# 20 THINGS I SAY TO MY 3 YEAR OLD ON A DAILY BASIS

by Aedin Collins

I'm not always a killjoy and I swear we do sometimes have the craic. Just not all the time as this list painfully demonstrates. Someone's gotta be the adult here right? Any of the following sound familiar to you?

1. "Get off the window sill/the table/your sister."

2. "Get out of the dishwasher."

3. "Where are your pants? Put on your pants!"

4. "No you can't have cake for breakfast."

5. "Where is Mammy's tweezers? expensive hand cream/new facial wash?"

6. "It's ten past five in the morning. No you can't watch Peppa Pig."

7. "It's quarter to six in the morning. No you can't watch Peppa Pig"

8. "It's quarter past six in the morning, No you can't..ah sod it, here's the iPad."

9. "I don't think your sister wants to go into the tumble dryer/oven/press/freezer."

10. "No you can't go outside in your slippers."

11. "But it's sweet potato/sweetcorn/peas-you loved them yesterday!"

12. "She's your sister and she loves you, that's why she wants to be close to you."

13. "It's 7:30. One more Peppa Pig and then bed."

14. "It's 7:45. One more Peppa Pig and then bed."

15. "It's 8:00. This is definitely the last Peppa Pig."

16. "I think the washing machine is ok for Duplo blocks, thanks."

17. "Take your pants off your head. We're going outside."

18. "Mammy would love to take you to Monkey Business for the third day in a row but I think they're closed today*."

19. "Look,this paper here would LOVE some colouring. I think the walls have had enough."

20. "Do you want the nightlight on? Ok, I'll turn it off. No you want it on? Ok. Off? Ok. On? Ok. Night night. Off? Ok…."

*This is an outright lie. They open seven days a week but there's only so much indoor play centre teeming with crazed toddlers and kids that Mammy can take.

## HILARIOUS PARENTING TWEET

"My four year old has just taken the remote control to the bathroom with her so that none of us can change the channel while she pees. Proud."

- Nikki Lawlor, @nikkilawlor85

# HOW TO GET YOUR MOM OUT OF THE BORING LADY STORE BY BOB ROSENBERG, 5 YEARS OLD

Interpreted by
Lisa Page Rosenberg

When you get in the Boring Lady Store, immediately start pulling on your mama's arm and repeatedly whisper, "Okay, okay, okay, okay. Let's go, let's go, let's go, let's go."

After your mom threatens to put you in a stroller, walk next to her quietly for a maximum of 40 seconds. Periodically ask if it's time to go yet.

She will hand some clothes to a lady who tells you that you're a "darling child." She says her name is Hillary and she is "starting a room" for your mom. You mention to Hillary that your mom already has a room and she shares it with Daddy. The grown-ups laugh at something.

Break free from mom's grasp. Pull a pile of yellow lady sweaters off of a table and on to the floor and yell, "Shiver me timbers!" This is not popular with your mama and she will have a "talk" with you by the big plant.

Your mom brings you with her into a tiny room with a big mirror on the wall. You look around and ask, "How come there's no potty in this potty?"

You are allowed to sit on the floor and go through the stuff in your mom's purse while she changes all of her clothes a bunch of times. (Except underpants.)

Hillary asks if we are, "doing okay in there" and you can take the opportunity to inform her that they "forgot the potty in this one."

Your mom will make you stand in a line to pay for one green sweater with some flowers on it. The line is long and you are not allowed to touch any of the things on the jewelry table and you are not allowed to move the rope thing that shows you where to stand and you are not allowed, not allowed, not allowed.

Break free from your mom as she gets to the front of the line. Sit in the big chair with the red flowers on it and wave.

Your mom will watch you as you stick your hand down your throat and then barf a little on a pillow with a bird picture on it.

Your mom will run to you in the big red flower chair and see your barf. She will pick up you and the bird pillow. She will buy the bird pillow instead of the green sweater and you will get to leave the store in a hurry.

She will explain to you that she hopes you like the trendy overpriced piece of c-r-a-p because it is going to be your wedding gift.

You don't know what that means but you get to go home now so it's good.

# UNDER THE WEATHER

"Mom? Since I'm staying home from school with this sore throat, we should go to the movies today."

"Are you kidding? No. We're not going to the movies."

"Can we go out for lunch?"

"No."

"Can I have a playdate later?"

"No."

"You're making being sick no fun at all."

– by Lisa Page Rosenberg

# TRIALS AND TRIBULATIONS OF THE TOOTH FAIRY

by Alison Huff

Well… there was that one time when the Tooth Fairy forgot to come. In my defense, it had been a very long day and I was physically exhausted. I went upstairs to bed that night and completely shirked my tooth thieving duties.

Morning came, as it tends to do, and I awoke to the screeching chorus of "HEY! THE TOOTH FAIRY DIDN'T TAKE MY TOOTH!"

Sleep still in my eyes, I threw on my robe and stumbled downstairs. Lo and behold, the Tooth Fairy had not come and my older daughter, Doom, was very distressed over this.

Thankfully, I'm a quick-thinking fairy. Even at 6:45 in the morning. And even before coffee. (I do have to wonder whether the *real* Tooth Fairy might have been spiritually guiding me somehow because let's face it, I'm lucky if I put my clothes on the right way that early in the morning, let alone being able to craft an explanation that actually makes sense.)

I rubbed my eyes. "Wow. Do you see how foggy it is outside? Look at that! I don't remember the last time I saw a fog so thick… geez. It's like we're living inside a cloud! I think maybe the Tooth Fairy just couldn't find our house in all that fog."

She seemed to accept my sound reasoning.

"Why don't you go put your tooth back on the night stand, and I'll make you and your sister some breakfast," I said.

Off she went, like nothing had happened. It began to get much lighter and brighter outside, and as they sat in the dining room together, eating oatmeal and bickering with each other, I formulated Phase Two of my little patch-up plan: a handwritten note that said, "Dear Doom, Sorry I was late! The fog light on my wand broke and I couldn't find your house until now. Love, The Tooth Fairy"

I slyly waltzed into the girls' bedroom while they ate, left the note (along with a five-spot because I felt so damned guilty) and pilfered the tooth.

I went about my morning routine, grabbing a cup of coffee and taking the dogs outside like I always do, raising no suspicion in any way.

# HILARIOUS PARENTING TWEETS

""Honey, I'll take the kids to school today if that's easi-"
[wife doesn't hear me, she's already headed to Starbucks, screaming "Sucker!"]"

## - Andy H. @AndyAsAdjective

"I've discovered the key to always having a hot cup of coffee!

Never have children."

## - Bad Parenting Moments, @BPMbadassmama

"Children: because who wants a hot meal anyway?"

## - Will Goldstein @willgoldstein

# A LETTER TO MY SEVEN YEAR OLD

- Andrea Mara

I think about how you said sorry so quickly when you knocked over the cereal box this morning, and my insides constrict. I told you it was fine, it was an accident – I brushed it away. But that doesn't change the fact that you rushed to say sorry – have I made you that way? Have I heaped these expectations on you, as the firstborn child?

I sit here thinking about giving you a big hug tomorrow morning when you wake up – I resolve to be better. To stop expecting so much, to remember that you're only seven. But I already know that the first time something comes up to distract me, I'll forget again. If you're slow to get ready for school in the morning, I know I'll rush you. If the end of your hair trails into your breakfast, I'll sigh and remind you to tie it up. If you disappear half way through breakfast to read your book, I'll probably snap at you. If your little brother does the same? There will be no snapping. Maybe exasperation, but he's only three. And that's not fair – in the bigger scheme of things, seven isn't so different to three. But you're the oldest, and more is expected. It's not fair. I mean to change, and I'll try to change, but I already know this is a life-long, or childhood-long road.

When you were three, as your brother is now, I expected too much. You were the big sister, no longer a baby. In hindsight, it was ridiculous, but I expected so much. He wanders off during mealtimes, helps himself to bread from the press, insists on putting on his own clothes no matter how long it takes, and always gets the toy – " Ah girls, he's only small, let him have it". You had no such allowances at three. I expected you to be grown-up, to do as you were told, to follow the rules. I expected too much.

When you were six, as your sister is now, you were the big girl. In school, articulate, capable of understanding every instruction. When you didn't, I grew frustrated. When you were cross – when you found it hard to adapt to change – I didn't understand. With your sister, I tiptoe. I anticipate change, I prepare her, and I praise her when she has a smooth transition. Why didn't I know to do that with you? I expected far too much.

And I already know, when your sister is seven, when your brother is seven, I'll have lowered my expectations. I won't see them as grown-up – I'll see them as they are now – children, still learning, little people for whom I need to make allowances.

And I need to realise that now – not in two or five years. That you're seven. And being the oldest doesn't make you older than your years. You can be grown-up – looking after your siblings, helping me with dishes, choosing your own clothes. And you can be little – chasing your brother around the table at breakfast time, not having a sense of urgency about the morning rush, letting your hair trail in your food. Of course you can. You're a little girl. And I need to remember that. I don't need to lower my expectations – you're perfect, just perfect as you are. I need to raise my expectations – of myself. And remember in the morning to hug you twice, and to tie your hair back for you.

## HILARIOUS PARENTING TWEET

"Was arguing with my 2 year old for 30 minutes about why he needs to wear his pants and now we're both sitting in our underwear eating donuts."

– Molly, @PaperWash

Sophie White
**(HerFamily)**

In former lives, Sophie White was an artist, a chef, a snowboarding and cycling enthusiast and a van-dwelling vagabond. Now she lives in a house with a man and a baby and showers more frequently. Sophie writes for HerFamily.ie as well as being a regular contributor to the Sunday Independent, writing interviews, reviews and style features. When she is not eating, she can mostly be found reading, bashfully re-watching Gilmore Girls or instigating human pyramids in the wee hours of the morning. And parenting.

HerFamily is a lifestyle parenting website offering realistic support, practical content and, sometimes, just a little light relief. Parents of Ireland catch up with us daily for realistic advice, news, tips and tricks, all wrapped up in a bit of wit and wisdom.

Follow her...
www.herfamily.ie

Alison Huff

**(Crumbsdown)**

Alison Huff is a writer who lives in the rural wilderness of bipolar northeastern Ohio, USA, with her husband, two daughters, and two dogs. She is a cadre writer for Bluntmoms.com, purveyor of satirical writing for MockMom, and a contributor to the anthologies, "Only Trollops Shave Above the Knee" (April, 2015) and "Martinis & Motherhood— Tales of Wonder, Woe and WTF?!" (June, 2015). Alison tweets @crumbsdown and shares her life stories on her blog, Please Stop Putting Crackers Down My Shirt.

Follow her...

www.crumbsdown.wordpress.com

Lisa Page Rosenberg
**(Smacksy)**

My kid is nine. His name is Bob. He talks a lot.
I write it down.
Lisa Page Rosenberg is a former writer/producer for television. Her stories have been included in essay collections, Listen to Your Mother, Moms Are Nuts, and A Letter to My Mom. Lisa is a frequent contributor at Huffington Post and a top 10 finalist in BlogHer Voice of the Year. Her daily family humor blog, smacksy.com, has been recognized by Parade Magazine and SheKnows. Lisa lives in Southern California with Mr. Rosenberg and their son Bob.

Follow her...
www.smacksy.com

Mary Widdicks
**(Outmanned Mommy)**

Once a cognitive psychologist in the field of memory, Mary Widdicks now spends the majority of her time trying to remember if she fed all her children each morning. The irony is not lost on her. Her writing has been featured on sites such as The Washington Post, Brain, Child Magazine, The Huffington Post, and Scary Mommy. She has been honored as a Voice of the Year by BlogHer in 2014 and 2015, and 2014 Badass Blogger of the Year by The Indie Chicks. In February of 2015 she gave birth to her first daughter and is now happily drowning in a sea of pink.

Follow her...
www.outmannedmommy.com

Rose Jacobs

**(When The Poop Hits The Propeller!)**

Rose Jacobs is a well respected Television Presenter and Producer for the Seven Network in Australia as well as being The Travel Expert for The Lifestyle Channels. Rose is a qualified Journalist and combines her love of travel, writing and her children into her blog with the aim of helping other parents travelling with kids with informative and entertaining advice.

Follow her...

www.poopypropeller.blogspot.com

Andrea Mara
**(Office Mum)**

Andrea Mara is a freelance writer and blogger, who lives in Dublin with her husband and three children. She attempts – often badly - to balance work and family, then lets off steam on her award-winning blog, 'Office Mum'.
Andrea has just completed her first suspense novel "The People Next Door" and is actively looking for an agent and publisher. When she's not keeping one eye on the kids, and the other on Twitter, she's furiously scribbling notes for her next book.

Follow her...
www.officemum.ie

Aedin Collins

**(Minis And Mum)**

Unlike some people who take to parenting like a duck to water, Aedín is just trying not to drown in a sea of sleepless nights, potty training disasters and general mayhem. Her motto though, is to just keep on swimming, fuelled on coffee and sticky toddler kisses. She chronicles her misadventures at award winning blog minisandmum.com, where she talks candidly about parenting, lifestyle and how Down syndrome ain't nothing but a (different) number (of chromosomes).

Follow her...
www.minisandmum.com

Mama Felton aka kelly
**(Mummy Moments)**

First time mum, blog writer, wife & working mama. Her blog is an honest account of life as a first time mum - the many highs, the few lows and the adventures in between.

Follow her...
www.mummymomentsdublin.com

Jennie Dennehy
**(Mummy Vs The World)**

I started my blog in February '15 and was delighted to win a Silver Award for 2nd Best Parenting Blog at the Blog Awards Ireland in October '15.

I have qualifications in English Literature and Journalism and worked for a leading cosmetics company for 8 years.

When I had my son, I was in the fortunate position that I could decide I no longer wanted to work full time and I currently juggle looking after him and blogging!

Follow her...
www.mummyvstheworld.com

Naomi Clarke
## (The Style Fairy)

Naomi Clarke, a first time mammy to Anabelle Ivy, is a blogger and fashion stylist. She is the creator of the multi award winning blog "The Style Fairy". Naomi who originally hails from Cavan now lives in Dun Laoghaire with her husband Cormac, her daughter and their crazy dog Oscar. After spending over two years living in both Sydney and Singapore and working in various fashion roles abroad, Naomi moved home in 2013 to launch her own business; The Style Fairy. The Style Fairy is a fashion, beauty and lifestyle blog which is all about real women and affordable fashion. Naomi also has her own brand of accessories and is set to launch her third collection in 2016. Since becoming a mammy, Naomi now shares personal insights into her joys and struggles in adjusting to her new role as a mum, all whilst trying to remain "somewhat" fashionable… Think running in heels, whilst also covered in baby vomit!

Follow her...
www.thestylefairy.ie

# RECORD SOME MEMORIES...

# ACKNOWLEDGEMENTS

**With special thanks to:**
Truzees editor and writer, Nikki Lawlor for understanding our vision for this book and contributing so much time into developing it.

To each and every contributor and to all who have featured in our book; for uniting together and allowing us to promote the untold stories of parenthood. Together, we have taken one step more towards assuring other parents they are doing just fine - whilst giving them a proper giggle along the way.

To Jeff Harvey for believing in this book and for creating beautiful photography that emulates our values perfectly.

To my mother who has gone above and beyond throughout her life to support me. Now I finally understand.

To my witty and beautiful son, who is the true inspirer of this book. I love you - with all my heart.

To my partner, my family, my friends and my colleagues in both Designhub and Truzees - all of whom I roped into helping me out on various occasions, thank you for all the support and for putting up with me. I don't know how you do it.

To the supportive community of women from "Acorns", "Going For Growth" and "Women's Inspire Network" - I hope every female entrepreneur finds their way to you.

- Angela